KIDS'
LETTERS
TO
PRESIDENT
REAGAN

"Kids' Letters to Presidents" books
compiled by Bill Adler:

Kids' Letters to President Kennedy

Dear President Johnson

Kids' Letters to President Carter

KIDS' LETTERS TO PRESIDENT REAGAN

Compiled and Edited by
BILL ADLER

Illustrations by SANDY HUFFAKER

Foreword by WILLARD SCOTT

M. EVANS AND COMPANY, INC.
NEW YORK

Library of Congress Cataloging in Publication Data

Main entry under title:

Kid's letters to President Reagan.

　1. Reagan, Ronald.　2. Children—Anecdotes,
facetiae, satire, etc.　I. Adler, Bill,
II. Huffaker, Sandy.
E877.2.K52　　973.927'092'4　　81-19472

ISBN 0-87131-370-7　　AACR2

M. Evans and Company, Inc.
216 East 49 Street
New York, New York 10017

Design by Ronald F. Shey

Manufactured in the United States of America

9 8 7 6 5 4 3 2 1

Editor's Note

This book is about a love affair—between young Americans and President Ronald Reagan.

From all over the country, youngsters have been writing to the President expressing their thoughts, dreams, hopes, ideas, complaints—but most of all their affection.

Obviously, without the young letter writers this book would not be possible, but we are also grateful to President Reagan. In capturing the fancy of Americans young and old, it is really he who has made this book possible.

Acknowledgments

We are most grateful to the many parents, grandparents, teachers, friends, and children who have sent us these letters to President Reagan so that we could share them with you.

The letters are as they were written—only the names have been changed to protect the innocent, and not so innocent.

Foreword

I love these letters!

Where else but in America could you find kids of all ages writing to the President to express their dreams, aspirations, affection, and even a complaint or two? Somewhere among these letter writers you may even find a future president or a secretary of state or a supreme court justice.

I never did write a letter to a president when I was a kid, but then again, Calvin Coolidge wasn't the sort of president who inspired letters.

Willard Scott
Of the *Today* Show

KIDS'
LETTERS
TO
PRESIDENT
REAGAN

Dear Mr. President,

Did Mrs. Reagan know you were going to be President when she married you?

Did you promise her you would be President so she would say yes?

Karen S.
Age 9
San Diego

Dear Mr. President,

I want to give you a kiss.

Love,
Susie S.
Age 7
Shaker Heights

P.S. I want to kiss Mrs. Reagan and your horse, too.

Dear Pres Reagan,

I saw you on the news on Channel 2, 4 and 7.

I hope you don't get tired running from Channel 2 to Channel 4 to Channel 7.

Your citizen,
Patty T.
Age 10
Montauk

Dear Mr. Pres Reagan,

Please send me a list of all the good things you have done so far as President.

Please send me the list right away because I have to write a story about you as President and I don't want to leave anything out.

> Your friend,
> *Laurence R.*
> Age 10
> Harrisburg

Dear Mr. President,

I love you.

I am 8.

Someday I want to be your First Lady.

> *Kathy S.*
> Age 8
> Los Angeles

Hi President!

I love you the best after my father.

> Love and kisses,
> *Natalie R.*
> Age 8
> Buffalo

Dear President Reagan,
    Please help with inflation.
    My allowance can't buy anything anymore.

                    Your citizen,
                    Thomas J.
                    Age 12
                    St. Louis

Dear Mr. President,
    I would like to shake your hand.
    I never shaked the hand of a President
before.

                    Love,
                    Alison E.
                    Age 8
                    Pawtucket

Dear Pres Reagan,
    Do you have to be the smartest person in the
U.S.A. to be President?
    I have read a lot in the history books about a
lot of Presidents and I'm not so sure.

                    Your friend,
                    George P.
                    Age 9
                    Philadelphia

Hi Mr. President!
  I think you're cute.
  I hope it is okay to call a President cute.

                    Love,
                    Natalie B.
                    Age 10
                    Pittsburgh

Dear Mr. Pres,

 Does a President have an expense account?
Who signs your expense account?

 My father has an expense account and he
cheats all the time.

> Yours truly,
> *Charles H.*
> Age 11
> Milwaukee

P.S. My father doesn't know I wrote this letter.

Dear Pres Reagan,

 I would like to send you a birthday card but I
don't know when it is.

 Send me the day of your birthday and I will
send you a 25 cents birthday card.

> *Gabriel H.*
> Age 9
> Philadelphia

Dear President Reagan,

 Do we have a lot of friends in the world or
mostly enemies?

> Your citizen,
> *James L.*
> Age 8
> Palm Springs

14

Dear Mr. President Reagan,
    I think you should send a woman into space.
Like my sister.

Love,
Haywood J.
Age 8
Norfolk

Dear President,
    I drew a picture of you.
    I hope you like the picture.
    I am a good American but not a terrific artist.

Your friend,
Pauline S.
Age 10
Santa Clara

Dear President Reagan,
    I hope you have a dog in the White House.
Every President should have a dog in the
White House even if he doesn't really want one.

Vicky M.
Age 9
Dallas

Dear President Reagan,
    I would like to be like you when I grow up.

                          Love,
                          Eric L.
                          Age 8
                          Ashland
P.S. My mother hopes I will change my mind.

Dear Pres Ronald Reagan,
    Is the U.S.A. broke?
    Thank you for the information.

                          Lawrence M.
                          Age 9
                          Rockville Centre

Dear Mr. Pres,
    I'm glad you are President instead of Jimmy
Carter because I like jelly beans better than
peanuts.

                          Your pal,
                          Ray V.
                          Age 9
                          Albany

16

✓Dear Pres Reagan,
    Is it safe to live in the White House?
    It isn't so safe to live in my house.

                        Your friend,
                        Katie W.
                        Age 9
                        Cambridge

Dear President Reagan,
    I like your smile.
    Do you have your own teeth?

                Love,
                Stacey R.
                Age 8
                Tacoma

Dear Pres Reagan,
    I'm glad the baseball strike is over.
    Now America is a great country again.

                A loyal American,
                Neil C.
                Age 9
                Waukegan

Dear Pres Reagan,
    I hope we have a woman President someday.

                Your friend,
                Hamilton J.
                Age 8
                Hartford
P.S. My father says that will be the end of the U.S.A.

Dear Mr. President,

I believe you should ban all the bombs.

If there is an atomic war, nothing will be left and the whole world will be very sorry because only ants and fish will be left.

A friend,
Molly D.
Age 8
Newark

Dear President,

My mother and father believe in equal rights for women but not for kids.

Your friend,
Justine H.
Age 10
Seattle

Dear Pres Ronald Reagan,

Did your mother know you were going to be President when you were 10 years old?

I am 10 years old and my mother doesn't think I will be President.

She doesn't think I will be good for much.

Harvey S.
Age 10
New Rochelle

Dear Mr. Pres Reagan,
        Can kids go on strike?
        The food in our lunchroom is terrible.

>   *Dana L.*
                                Age 10
                                Atlanta

Dear Mr. President Reagan,
        Please write me a letter even if you have
nothing to say.

                                Pauline H.
                                Age 12
                                Detroit

Dear Mr. Reagan,
        What happens to a President when he
becomes an ex-President?
        I think you should find out because someday
you will be an ex.

                                Love,
                                Stacey H.
                                Age 10
                                Newark

Dear Pres Reagan,

I don't think people should be allowed to drive their car unless they use their seat belt.

You should make it a law even if you don't have to drive your own car and you have the Secret Service to keep you safe without a seat belt.

> Your citizen,
> *Ila H.*
> Age 10
> Skokie

Dear Mr. President,

I hope Mrs. Reagan is the first woman President of the United States.

You should try and help Mrs. Reagan to be the first woman President of the U.S. even if it means you have to find another job.

Respectfully,
Tracy J.
Age 9
Wyndham

Dear President Reagan:

I heard your speech on TV.

I liked it a lot because you didn't use big words.

Your fan,
Jason H.
Age 8
Las Vegas

Dear Mr. President Ronald Reagan:

I think you are the handsomest President except for JFK and General Grant.

Yours truly,
Arnold H.
Age 9
Tulsa

Dear President Reagan:

You are the first President I ever wrote to.

I hope you write back because if you don't I'll never write to a President again.

Your friend,
Barbara R.
Age 8
New Haven

Dear Mr. President Reagan:

Could you please tell me if it is good or bad for the country that you are President?

Thank you.

Donald W.
Age 7
Brooklyn

Dear Mr. President,

I would like a picture of you when you were a kid.

Here is a picture of me when I was a kid.

Love,
Virginia R.
Age 11
Philadelphia

Dear President Reagan,
    I would like to work at the White House after school.
    I could do jobs for you and Mrs. Reagan that the F.B.I. won't do for you.

                              Your American,
                              Lloyd P.
                              Age 10
                              Baltimore

Dear Mr. President,
    Are you a war President or a peace President?

                              Respectfully,
                              Amanda S.
                              Age 10
                              Terre Haute

Dear President,
    Is it hard to be Pres of the U.S.A.?
    Would it be easier to be a dictator?

                              An American,
                              Lorna S.
                              Age 10
                              Madison

Dear Pres Reagan,

Are you the first President that ate jelly beans?

I never read that George Washington liked jelly beans.

Harvey M.
Age 9
Cambridge

Dear Mr. President Reagan,

Do women have more rights than other people?

Me and my friend will be women when we grow up.

Sincerely,
Nancy T.
Age 8
Kansas City

Dear President,

What do you like better?

To be President of the United States or Gov of California?

Your friend,
Frank S.
Age 9
Wheeling

Dear President Reagan,

I like your movies a lot and I'm not even a Republican.

Sally F.
Age 9
Fresno

Dear Mr. Pres,
     You have the Secret Service and the F.B.I. to protect you.
     All I have is my dog, Kelly.
     And Kelly is afraid of cats.

> Love,
> *Wallace R.*
> Age 8
> Charleston

Dear Mr. Pres,
     I read in the paper that you may stop the student loan program.
     I hope you don't do that.
     I need a student loan to go to college so I can be a doctor someday.

> *Jocelyn L.*
> Age 10
> Jenkintown

P.S. I won't charge you when I am a doctor.

Dear Pres,
     I love you and the Pope the best.

> *Olga R.*
> Age 8
> Boston

Dear Pres Reagan,

    Could you please send me the names of some cheap colleges?

    I can't pay to go to the other kind.

> *Raphael C.*
> Age 12
> Carson City

Dear President Reagan,

    There is too much air pollution.

    We have too much air pollution because there are too many autos.

    We should stop the cars and have everybody ride bikes or roller skates.

> *Peter W.*
> Age 9
> San Bernardino

Dear Mr. President,

    Please do something about the cost of food.

    My mom can only buy Twinkies once a month.

> Love,
> *Alexandra M.*
> Age 10
> Tulane

Dear Mr. Reagan,
    Were there ever any other Presidents in your family?

                        Love,
                        Erica B.
                        Age 9
                        New Hope

Dear Mr. President Reagan,
   I am going to be President of the U.S.A.
   My girlfriend, Alyce, is going to be Vice-President.

> *Gregg W.*
> Age 9
> Alexandria

Dear Mr. President,
   I would like to be President because the President gets to travel a lot for free and I can't even go to Philadelphia by bus.

> Love,
> *Jeanine W.*
> Age 11
> Trenton

✓ Dear President Reagan,
   How many bathrooms are there in the White House?
   There are two bathrooms in my house and we are 5 kids and my mother, my father, my Aunt Sara, my Uncle Jeff and the cats.

> Yours truly,
> *Teddy H.*
> Age 9
> Minneapolis

Dear Pres Reagan,

I hope you don't take too much money from the arts.

If there isn't enough money for the arts my church may never be able to do the Nativity next Christmas.

Love,
Paul W.
Age 11
Hasbrouck Heights

Dear President Reagan,

I think someday you will be called the jelly bean President.

Love,
William H.
Age 10
Bronx

Dear Pres Reagan,

I hope my teacher Miss Smith is teacher of the year.

Could you please help Miss Smith to be teacher of the year?

Miss Smith is a great teacher even when she is in a bad mood.

Best wishes,
Joanna F.
Age 10
Salt Lake City

Dear Pres Reagan,

Do you play golf?

I've never seen any pictures of you playing golf.

Are you the first President that doesn't play golf?

Sincerely,
Dana F.
Age 10
Albuquerque

Dear Mr. President,

I'm sorry you couldn't go to Prince Charles's wedding.

I promise to invite you to my wedding someday.

Love,
Mindy H.
Age 9
Fargo

P.S. Mrs. Reagan can come too.

Dear Mr. Pres Reagan,

I go to church every Sunday.

I pray for America and my little league baseball team.

Theodore C.
Age 9
Oklahoma City

Dear Pres Reagan,

Could you please help my father with his taxes?

After he pays his taxes he doesn't have enough money left even to feed the canary.

Love,
Patricia R.
Age 8
Birmingham

Dear President,
    I am 8.
    Please don't have any war because I want to
be 10 someday.

                                    Love,
                                    Patricia Z.
                                    Age 8
                                    Wallingford

Dear Mr. President,
        Are you a male chauvinist?
        My big sister wants to know.
                                    Your pal,
                                    Ellen C.
                                    Age 10
                                    Santa Fe

Dear Mr. President,
        I hope a woman is President of the U.S.A.
        The reason I think a woman should be
President of the U.S.A. is they can't do much
worse.

                                    Your friend,
                                    Paula G.
                                    Age 10
                                    Princeton

34

Dear President Reagan,

My father is a good American but sometimes he doesn't have enough money to pay his taxes.

Please don't get mad at my father.

He is a veteran.

> Your pal,
> *Sanford B.*
> Age 9
> Wausau

Dear Mr. Pres,

What will you do when you are ex-President Reagan?

Will you be an actor again?

Maybe now you will win an Academy Award because you have had a lot of practice as President.

> Your friend,
> *Serena C.*
> Age 9
> San Francisco

Dear Pres Reagan,

Does the government tell the truth?

My brother isn't so sure.

> Your American,
> *Desmond K.*
> Age 8
> Taos

Dear Mr. President,

I think before we send another man to the moon we should fix the subways in New York.

Yours truly,
David J.
Age 9
Manhattan

Dear Mr. President,

How much rent do you pay in the White House?

We pay $315 a month.

Do you have a nice landlord at the White House?

Our landlord hates everybody.

Sincerely,
Deidre D.
Age 9
Chicago

Dear Pres Reagan,

Do you ever get mad?

My father says you never get mad except at the Channel 2 news.

Your friend,
Annie W.
Age 10
Philadelphia

Dear President Reagan,

I hope you don't build the neutron bomb.

I think we should get rid of all bombs.

Even the water bombs my Uncle Steve likes to make for fun.

Your citizen,
David R.
Age 8
Bellevue

Dear President,
        Hello.
        I am Stevie.
        I am 6.
        My mommy wrote this letter for me.
        I want to be Pres.
        But I can't be Pres yet because I'm not
allowed to cross the street by myself yet.

                        Love,
                        Stevie R.
                        Age 6
                        Orlando

Dear Mr. President,
        I am glad you are the President but I don't
know why.

                        William Z.
                        Age 8
                        Houston

Dear Mr. President,
        You are the most popular person in the
Bronx after Reggie Jackson.
        If he doesn't hit 300 this year you will be the
most popular.

                        Ronald N.
                        Age 10
                        Bronx

Dear Pres Reagan,
✔ Did we win World War II or did the
Japanese?
    I would like a true answer.

> *Herbert C.*
> Age 9
> Miami

Dear Mr. President,
    What is your favorite city in the U.S.A.?
    What city were you born in?
    What city do you hate the most?
    Who is the greatest American besides you?
    Please write me back.

> *Georgia B.*
> Age 8
> Wheeling

Dear President Reagan,
✓ Someday I would like to visit the White
House but I want to go to Disneyland first.

> Love,
> *Norman K.*
> Age 9
> Buffalo

Dear Pres Ronald Reagan,

What time do you get up in the morning?

I guess a President can sleep as late as he wants.

My mother makes me get up at 7:00 A.M.

Your friend,
Mark L.
Age 9
Chevy Chase

Dear Mr. President,

I hope you live forever and my father said you already have.

Christopher W.
Age 8
Trenton

Dear Mr. President,

Please come to Grand Rapids when you aren't too busy with Russians and the baseball strike.

Carole W.
Age 9
Grand Rapids

Dear Pres Reagan,
    I like your smile.
    Are you always happy even when you read
the newspaper?

Love,
Caryn H.
Age 9
Raleigh

Dear Pres Ronald Reagan,
   I think you should make a law against dentists.
   Please do it before Tuesday.
   That's when I have to go to Dr. Pearl again.

> Lynn T.
> Age 9
> Fort Benning

Dear Mr. President,
   I am against marijuana but if people want to smoke you should let them do it.
   America is a free country even for people who smoke marijuana or drink beer.

> Your friend,
> Felicia J.
> Age 10
> Englewood

Dear Pres Reagan,
   I saw a picture of you on a horse.
   Do you think the horse knows you are a President?

> A citizen,
> Scott H.
> Age 8
> Weston

Dear Pres Ronald Reagan,

I think we should do more for the American Indian.

The Indians were the first people in America and if we didn't have the Indians America would be just a place where there were only buffaloes.

Thank you for helping the Indians.

> *Andrew M.*
> Age 10
> Joplin

Dear Pres Reagan,

✓ Someday the U.S.A. will run out of water.

We should stop wasting water or soon all we will have to drink is Coke and 7-Up.

> Your citizen,
> *Beth J.*
> Age 11
> Miami

Dear Mr. Pres,

Why do we have to pay taxes?

Could you please send me a postcard and tell me why?

> Your friend,
> *Katherine R.*
> Age 8
> Middletown

Dear Mr. Pres,

How long have you and Mrs. Reagan been married?

My mother and father have been married for 22 years.

Your citizen,
Ellen H.
Age 9
Albany

P.S. My father isn't a President but my mother still loves him.

Dear Mr. President,

Are you for or against the people?

Respectfully,
Katie H.
Age 9
Canton

Dear Mr. President,

I am glad my mother and father voted for you.

My grandmother didn't vote for you because the last President she voted for was President Truman.

Your friend,
Bruce W.
Age 10
Raleigh

44

Dear Mr. President,
My birthday is July 21.
Please make it a national holiday.

                    Your friend,
                    Lewis B.
                    Age 10
                    New York

Dear Pres Ronald Reagan,
    Do you like to jog?
    I like to jog.
    Jogging is very good for you.
    You should jog when you are not on TV or
working at the White House.

                        Love,
                        George K.
                        Age 9
                        Clearwater

Dear Mr. President,
    The honest citizens need more policemen.
    We don't have enough policemen in Buffalo.
    There are more crooks than cops.

                        Your citizen,
                        Jesse G.
                        Age 10
                        Buffalo

Dear Pres Ronald Reagan,
    I would like a picture of your horse.
    I already have enough pictures of Presidents.

                        Faith K.
                        Age 10
                        Bloomington

46

Dear Mr. President,

Did you spank your kids?

I hope not.

Because if the Pres of the U.S.A. didn't spank his kids then my father won't spank me.

Love,
Ellis M.
Age 8
Little Rock

Dear Pres Reagan,

Is it harder to be an actor in Hollywood or an actor as President?

John R.
Age 9
Oakland

Dear Mr. Pres:

✓ My mom looks like Mrs. Reagan.

You should meet my mom sometime.

She is very nice.

My mom is the First Lady in our house.

Gordon P.
Age 8
Winnetka

Dear Mr. President,
    Everybody likes you.
    Even the Democrats.
            Love,
            Terry A.
            Age 8
            Farmingdale

✔Dear Mr. President,
    Do you believe in heaven?
    I hope you do because when you go to
heaven then you can see all the other Presidents
who went to heaven except the Presidents who
didn't.
                Love,
                Linda K.
                Age 7
                Hollywood

Dear Mr. President,
    Will you run for President again?
    I hope Mrs. Reagan lets you do it.
                Love,
                Amy B.
                Age 8
                Baltimore

Dear President Reagan,
 Are Americans too fat?
 Please help the fat Americans like my Uncle
Michael.

Love,
Vicky G.
Age 9
Anderson

Dear Pres Reagan,

My mother and father like you very much.
Their name is Mr. and Mrs. Carlson.

They are good citizens and pay their taxes
and never break the law.

You should invite them to the White House
sometime when you want to meet average
Americans.

Sincerely,
Sylvia C.
Age 10
Milwaukee

Dear Mr. President,

What is your favorite TV program?

I would like to know so I can watch the same
TV program as the President of the U.S.A.

Your friend,
Brooke A.
Age 9
Minneapolis

Dear Mr. President,

Are you a good father?

I guess the President has to be a good father
because if the President isn't a good father then
nobody else will be a good father.

Thank you for being a good father.

Love,
Terence H.
Age 8
Jacksonville

50

Dear President Reagan,

How much vacation does a President get?

My father is a fireman and he gets 2 weeks vacation.

But I guess a President gets more vacation because a fireman works hard and puts out fires but a President has to be ready all the time even when he is sleeping.

An American,
Lloyd T.
Age 9
Boston

Dear Pres Reagan,

I live in Washington, D.C. like you and I deliver newspapers.

I would like to deliver newspapers to the White House.

I am very nice and I can get there every morning before you and Mrs. Reagan have your orange juice.

Your friend,
Allen H.
Age 9
Washington

Dear Pres Reagan,

I am happy there will be a woman on the Supreme Court.

But I don't think she should have to wear a black robe.

Maybe she could wear a robe that is a pretty color.

Love,
Helaine L.
Age 11
Boston

Dear Sir,

I read you have your own theater in the White House.

Now I know why you wanted to be President.

> Mitchell C.
> Age 10
> New York

Dear President Reagan,

I'm glad a lot of people voted for you.

Please don't be mad at the people who didn't vote for you.

> Love,
> Veronica H.
> Age 9
> Chicago

Dear President,

How would you look with a mustache?
I drawed a picture of you with a mustache.
I hope Mrs. Reagan likes it.

> Love,
> Marianne T.
> Age 8
> Valdosta

Dear Mr. Pres,

How much do you weigh?

Do you weigh more or less than Abraham Lincoln?

> Michael G.
> Age 9
> Dayton

✓ Dear Mr. President,

Why did they paint the White House white? Couldn't they get any other paint?

Could you please have somebody important answer?

> Thank you,
> Elizabeth Y.
> Age 9
> Lexington

Dear Pres Reagan,

Could you please get my father a good job?

All the companies he works for always go out of business and the government never goes out of business.

> Randall P.
> Age 9
> Brooklyn

54

Dear Mr. President,
    I watch the news on TV every night so I can
see you and Dan Rather.

> A friend,
> *Tanya J.*
> Age 10
> Portland

Dear President,

What is the safest city in the United States? I think maybe we should move.

Your citizen,
Amy C.
Age 9
Los Angeles

Dear Mister President,

I hope you have time to read my letter.

I know a President is very busy so maybe Mrs. Reagan could read my letter for you.

Love,
Ralph L.
Age 8
Gainesville

Dear President,

If you need a good Secret Service agent you should get Clint Eastwood.

Stacy W.
Age 9
Cheyenne

Dear Mr. Reagan,

Who was your favorite actress when you were an actor?

Was she as good an actress as Mrs. Reagan?

Love,
Diane P.
Age 9
Palo Alto

Dear Pres Reagan,

You wear nice clothes.

I think you dress better than Pres Carter or Pres Herbert Hoover.

Your citizen,
Scott A.
Age 10
Des Moines

Dear Mr. President,

I'm glad you don't smoke.

I would never want to have a President who smokes.

Your friend,
Kate Y.
Age 10
Brooklyn

P.S. I hope you don't drink or eat chocolate.

Dear Pres Reagan,

I saw one of your movies on TV last night.

I liked the picture a lot except they didn't call you Mr. President.

Love,
Jane P.
Age 9
Joplin

Dear Mr. President Reagan,

If you weren't President of the United States, I wish it could be Prince Charles.

Sincerely yours,
Vicky B.
Age 8
Nutley

Dear Pres Reagan,

I like you on TV a lot even when you are on TV instead of the good programs.

Respectfully,
Julian D.
Age 9
Norwich

Dear President Reagan,

Mrs. Reagan is too beautiful just to be a First Lady.

You should let her be in the movies like Bo Derek.

Love,
Tracey G.
Age 10
Las Vegas

Dear Pres Reagan,

I think you are the best President since Jimmy Carter.

A loyal citizen,
Jenny H.
Age 11
Muncie

Dear President,

We would like you to come to our house for dinner.

Could you please come on Friday night?

That's the night mom always makes fried chicken.

Yours,
Marjorie C.
Age 9
Lincoln

Dear President Reagan,

I've seen you on TV a lot since you became President.

You are a great actor.

Best wishes,
Coleen W.
Age 9
Bridgeport

Dear Pres,
    I live in Oklahoma City.
    Could you please come to Oklahoma City?
    There are very nice people in Oklahoma City.
    Even the Democrats.

                                A friend,
                                Donna C.
                                Age 8
                                Oklahoma City

Dear Mr. Pres Reagan,
    I think you should get a medal.

                                Your pal,
                                Mike G.
                                Age 8
                                Poughkeepsie
P.S. If the U.S. won't give you a medal, my Cub
Scout troop will give you one.

Dear Mr. President,
    What does a President do when he isn't on
television?

                                Thank you,
                                Donald S.
                                Age 10
                                Anderson

Dear Mr. President Reagan,

I think you should make a law that nobody can smoke cigarettes.

Please start with my mother.

Sandra H.
Age 10
Atlantic City

Dear Mr. Pres,

I believe you are the most popular President since Napoleon.

Love,
Melissa R.
Age 9
Milwaukee

Dear Mr. President,

I would like to be in the President's cabinet.

I would like to be Secretary of State or Secretary of Defense or any other jobs where you need help right away.

Your citizen,
Bobby D.
Age 10
Salt Lake City

Dear Pres Ronald Reagan,
    I read that your son Ron is a ballet dancer.
    I want to be a ballet dancer when I grow up
or maybe a football player.

> Your friend,
> *Peter F.*
> Age 10
> Redondo Beach

Dear Mr. Reagan,

Do you wear your cowboy boots in the White House?

I think you should wear your cowboy boots in the White House because some people like cowboys better than Presidents.

Love,
Jay K.
Age 8
Utica

Dear Pres Reagan,

I would like to go into the army someday if I can be a general.

Please take my name.

Yours truly,
Frederick P.
Age 10
Wilmington

Dear Mr. Pres,

Do you know Brooke Shields?

Love,
Agatha R.
Age 9
Gainesville

Dear Mr. Pres,

I would like to fly the President's plane to Los Angeles because I want to visit my grandmother and I don't have any money for an airplane ticket.

Your friend,
Sandy M.
Age 10
New York

Dear President,

I would like to see you in the Rose Garden at the White House but I'm allergic.

Love,
William J.
Age 8
Phoenix

Dear Mr. President,

My school orchestra would like to come and play for you and Mrs. Reagan at the White House.

I hope we can come soon.

Sincerely yours,
Abby B.
Age 12
Boston

P.S. We don't play too loud.

Dear President Reagan,

Please send me a letter and a picture.

Love,
Norman M.
Age 9
Fort Meyers

P.S. It won't cost you any money because a President doesn't have to pay for his own stamp.

Dear President Reagan,

Please send me some of your jelly beans.
I never had a President's jelly beans before.

Love,
Jennifer K.
Age 9
Hartford

Dear Mr. President,

You should get Superman to work for the U.S.A.

If we had Superman we wouldn't have to worry about anybody.

Your citizen,
Aaron P.
Age 8
Cleveland

Dear Mr. Pres,

My mother and father are divorced.

My mother is a Democrat and my father is a Republican.

Maybe that's why they are divorced.

Your citizen,
Bruce L.
Age 9
Hawthorne

Dear Mr. President,

    I think a lot of people were surprised when you became President, especially Jimmy Carter.

> Your friend,
> *David Y.*
> Age 10
> Portland

Dear President Reagan,

    We have a lot of trouble in our family.

    My mother doesn't feel so good and my father just lost his job and my grandfather is in the hospital.

    Everything else is okay except the dog hates the cat.

> Your citizen,
> *Ray G.*
> Age 9
> Abilene

Dear President,

    You and Teddy Roosevelt are the best cowboy Presidents.

> A student,
> *Paul H.*
> Age 11
> Kansas City

Dear Pres Ronald Reagan,
    I am going to be a Republican when I grow up.
    Right now I'm only a Boy Scout.

                        Your friend,
                        Albert W.
                        Age 9
                        Staten Island

Dear Pres Reagan,
    Who was your favorite President when you were a child?
    I would like to know even if it was Calvin Coolidge.

                        Jerome L.
                        Age 11
                        Minneapolis

Dear Mr. Pres,
    If you have a draft for the army, please take my big brother first.

                        Your friend,
                        Lloyd G.
                        Age 7
                        Brookline

Dear Pres Reagan,
>What size sweater do you wear?
>My mother is making you a surprise.
>>Love,
>>*Barbara R.*
>>Age 10
>>New York

Dear Sir,
>My girlfriend is Barbara.
>I am going to marry Barbara someday but first I want to make a million dollars.
>Then I will marry Barbara when I am 18.
>>Your citizen,
>>*Roy M.*
>>Age 9
>>Bethesda

Dear Pres Ronald Reagan,
>I would like to be Pres of the U.S.A. for a day.
>>Thank you,
>>*Charles C.*
>>Age 9
>>Newton

P.S. If a day is too much 5 seconds is okay.

Dear President,
    Do Russians go to heaven?
               Grace K.
               Age 8
               Tuscaloosa

Dear Mr. President,

Does Mrs. Reagan know any White House secrets?

My father tells my mother everything.

Your pal,
Emanuel J.
Age 9
Syracuse

Dear President,

I think George Washington would have liked you.

Daniel R.
Age 9
Honolulu

Dear Pres Reagan,

I would like to bring my puppy to the White House.

You don't have to worry. He is paper trained.

Love,
Leslie H.
Age 9
Wilkes-Barre

Dear Mister President,

I would like a souvenir from the White House.

Anything would be okay except the desk.

Robin G.
Age 9
Green Bay

Dear Mr. President Reagan,

I would like to be your best friend.

I never had a best friend who was a President before.

Thank you.
Cara M.
Age 8
Wilton

Dear Mr. President,

Do you need a good cook in the White House? My mother is a great cook.

Love,
Sandra R.
Age 8
Sausalito

P.S. I hope Mrs. Reagan won't get mad about my letter.

Dear Pres Reagan,

   I would like to live in Washington, D.C. but only if I can be President.

> Your citizen,
> *Alison H.*
> Age 8
> Scranton

Dear Mr. Pres,

   Could you please help my father with his parking ticket.

   He forgot he was parked in the wrong place. Thank you.

> Love,
> *Loren R.*
> Age 8
> Cincinnati

P.S. He didn't mean it.

Dear Mr. Pres Reagan:

   I have a question.

   Did you want to be President because you never got an Academy Award?

> Love,
> *Cynthia P.*
> Age 10
> Cincinnati

Dear President,
    I hope they give you a monument in Washington like Lincoln and Jefferson.

An American,
Charles G.
Age 10
Portland

P.S. You will have to wait.

Dear Mr. Pres Reagan,

I thank God every day that you are Pres of the U.S.A.

> *Sherry L.*
> Age 8
> Shaker Heights

Dear Pres Ronald Reagan,

✓ Do you have any bad habits?

My mother said I shouldn't write and ask a President if he has any bad habits.

But everybody has bad habits except dead people.

> Your friend,
> *Edwin F.*
> Age 9
> Nashville

Dear Mr. President,

I would like you to come to New York and march in the St. Patrick's Day parade.

You don't have to be Irish to march in the St. Patrick's Day parade.

You just have to like parades.

> Your citizen,
> *Sean J.*
> Age 9
> New York

Dear Sir,

I am sending you a picture of my sister.

My sister is very pretty and she would like to find a boyfriend.

I am sending the picture to you because maybe you know a boyfriend for my sister because the President knows everybody.

Thank you,
George B.
Age 8
Newark

Dear Pres Reagan,

I think Barbara Walters should be Secretary of State.

Gloria S.
Age 10
Teaneck

Dear Pres Ronald Reagan,

I would like to study in school how to be President of the U.S.A.

Could you please tell me what to study?

My best subject is art.

Your friend,
Eric W.
Age 9
Wilmette

Dear Pres Reagan,

Do you and Mrs. Reagan fight?

My mother and father fight all the time and my father is only a bus driver.

Yours truly,
Seth C.
Age 10
Boston

Hi Mr. President!

I hope you make a law so people can't buy guns.

If there weren't so many guns not so many people would get killed.

Thank you,
Alex C.
Age 9
Baltimore

P.S. The F.B.I. can carry guns.

Dear Pres Reagan,

I am a loyal American.
Please take my name.

Your citizen,
Richard H.
Age 10
Chicago

Dear Pres Reagan,

I want to be famous and rich when I grow up.

Should I be President of the U.S.A. or like John Travolta?

Thank you.

Roger K.
Age 10
Tampa

Dear Pres Reagan,

How do you like Washington?
How does Mrs. Reagan like Washington?
Do you miss your ranch?
Do you like horses better than Congress?

> Your fan,
> *Perry W.*
> Age 9
> Cleveland

Dear Mr. Pres Reagan,

Have you ever been to New Rochelle?
Please come to New Rochelle.
Then you will go into the history books as the first President to visit New Rochelle.

> Love,
> *Christopher C.*
> Age 9
> New Rochelle

Dear Pres Ronald Reagan,

My class voted you the best American President of 1981.

> Sincerely,
> *Elizabeth H.*
> Age 9
> Detroit

Dear Mr. Pres,

I saw a picture of you and Mrs. Reagan wearing jeans on your ranch.

Do you ever wear jeans at the White House?

Your friend,
Robert K.
Age 10
Boston

P.S. I think jeans are okay at the White House.

Dear Pres Reagan,

Do you think the end of the world will ever come?

Will you be President then?

Your citizen,
Lester K.
Age 10
Altoona

Dear President,

Did you really play football for Notre Dame? I saw you do it on the late show.

Yours truly,
Valerie H.
Age 9
Hollywood

Dear Pres Reagan,

I would like to come and take your picture at the White House.

I have an instant camera so I can take your picture quick and you won't even have to waste any time from the big deals in Washington.

Thank you.

Franklin G.
Age 9
Middlebury

Dear President Reagan,

Do you watch the Johnny Carson show?

He says some funny things about you and Mrs. Reagan.

Love,
Sheila B.
Age 8
La Jolla

Dear Pres Reagan and Mrs. Reagan:

I don't think you will like living in Washington as much as California.

There are no movie stars in Washington.

Your friend,
Laurie G.
Age 8
Atlanta

Dear Pres Reagan,

    What does Mrs. Reagan do all day?

    My mother isn't the First Lady so she doesn't do much except take care of us 7 kids and the 3 dogs and the 5 cats.

> Love,
> *Hilda W.*
> Age 8
> St. Louis

Dear President Reagan:

I hope you do something for women when you are President.

I am only a kid but someday I will be a woman, too.

> Your citizen,
> *Amy L.*
> Age 9
> Los Angeles

Dear President Ronald Reagan:

I would like to visit you in the White House someday when you aren't too busy with the rest of the country.

> Yours truly,
> *Bobby W.*
> Age 8
> San Francisco

Dear Mr. President Reagan:

I saw a picture of Mrs. Reagan on a horse.

I don't think the First Lady should ride on a horse.

I think she should ride in a big car instead.

> A citizen,
> *Stephanie H.*
> Age 8
> Detroit

Dear Pres Ronald Reagan,
   What is your favorite sport?
   Is it tennis?
   Is it baseball?
   Is it football?
   Is it basketball?
   Is it soccer?
   Is it golf?
   Is it swimming?
   My favorite sport is all of them.

                              Your pal,
                              Parker A.
                              Age 10
                              Westport

Dear Sir:
   Why does the U.S. Mail take so long?
   I think we should bring back the pony
express.

                              Roberto D.
                              Age 9
                              Chester

Hi Mr. Prez,
   You are the most famous person in the U.S.A.
except for Dan Rather.

                              Cindy J.
                              Age 10
                              Hartford

Dear President Reagan,
   I would like to read the story of your life if it isn't too boring.

Your fan,
Aaron R.
Age 10
Seattle

Dear President Ronald Reagan,

What do you like best about being President?

The thing I would like best about being President is the push-button phone on the President's desk.

>Love,
>*Holly M.*
>Age 9
>Cincinnati

Dear Pres Reagan,

I read in the newspaper that you used to be a Democrat.

Why did you become a Republican?

My father has always been a loyal American except when he voted for Eisenhower, Nixon and you.

>A citizen,
>*Samantha R.*
>Age 11
>San Antonio

Dear Mr. President,

Who is the boss of the U.S.A.?

You or Mrs. Reagan?

>Love,
>*Elaine J.*
>Age 9
>Evanston

Dear Mr. President Reagan,
Please send me your picture.

Love,
Laura J.
Age 9
San Diego

P.S. I will send you my picture when the dentist takes the braces off my teeth.

Dear Pres,
What is your favorite food?

I am doing a report for school on important facts about important people.

Peggy F.
Age 10
Chicago

Dear Mr. President Ronald Reagan,
I hope you will read my letter even if you are busy.

You should read what the people have to say even the kids.

Love,
Jay H.
Age 9
Grand Rapids

Dear Mr. Pres,

I guess because you are President you know everybody.

Do you know Miss Piggy and the Muppets?

Love,
Ann D.
Age 8
Nashville

Dear Pres Reagan,

Does Mrs. Reagan call you Ronnie or Mr. President?

Your citizen,
Aaron P.
Age 11
Seattle

Dear Mister President,

I hope we never have a war.
Grownups should be like kids.
Kids never have a real war.

Love,
Marie C.
Age 10
Corpus Christi

Dear President Reagan:

Why did you want to be President?
I would rather be an actor.
Actors make more money than Presidents.

Your citizen,
Wally B.
Age 11
Houston

Dear President Ronald Reagan:
 I would like to be your pen pal.

>Your friend,
>*Martin H.*
>Age 10
>Dallas

P.S. Please send me $3.00 for postage stamps.

Dear President Reagan:
 I hope you have fun when you are President.
 I don't think Pres Carter had as much fun as when he was a peanut farmer.

>Your friend,
>*Aaron H.*
>Age 10
>Memphis

Dear Pres Reagan:
 How did you win the election?
 I have run for President of my class 3 times and I haven't won yet.

>Sincerely yours,
>*Carl H.*
>Age 10
>Seattle

Dear Pres Ronald Reagan:
    I hope you will be President in 1990.
    I will be 18 then and I can vote for you.
                            Stephanie L.
                            Age 8
                            Chicago

Dear Mr. President,
    How come you don't have any gray hair?
    My father is 40 and he is already bald and
gray.
                            Your friend,
                            Cheryl H.
                            Age 10
                            Newark

Dear President Reagan:
    My mother and father voted for you even
though they saw all your old pictures.
                            Yours truly,
                            Bruce G.
                            Age 9
                            Seattle

Dear Pres Reagan:
2. Which President was the best actor besides you?

> Love,
> *Debbie K.*
> Age 9
> New York

Dear President Ronald Reagan:

I think Mrs. Reagan is very pretty.

Was she a movie star like you or was she just another woman?

Sincerely,
Denise K.
Age 8
San Diego

Dear President Reagan:

I hope you like to live in the White House.

I live in a white house too but sometimes the roof leaks.

Your friend,
Arthur L.
Age 9
Cincinnati

Dear President Reagan:

Did you want to be President when you were a kid?

I am 10 and I still don't know what I want to be.

Your friend,
Bruce W.
Age 10
Chicago

P.S. Maybe I will know when I'm 11.

Dear President Reagan:

Please write and tell me what the President does all day and I will write you back and tell you what I do all day.

Yours truly,
Martin G.
Age 9
Atlanta

Dear President Reagan:

Are you the first President to ride a horse since George Washington?

Love,
Victoria J.
Age 9
Miami

Dear Mr. Reagan:

My best friend Arthur says that the reason you got elected President was because you really knew John Wayne.

I thought you would want this information.

A citizen,
Michael B.
Age 9
Pittsburgh

Dear President Reagan:
    I want to be President of the U.S.A.
    Please send me a letter so I will know how to do it.

                  Thank you,
                  William H.
                  Age 10
                  St. Louis

P.S. I will be a good President.

Dear President Reagan:
    I think the whole U.S.A. loves you a lot.
    So do I.

                  Your citizen,
                  Karen J.
                  Age 8
                  Miami

Dear President Reagan:
    I would like to ride in the President's airplane.
    Thank you very much.
    I would like to ride from my house to school.

                  Gloria G.
                  Age 8
                  St. Louis

Dear Pres Reagan,
I would like your fingerprints.

Dexter H.
Age 9
Knoxville

Dear Pres Reagan:

I hope Mrs. Reagan likes it in the White House.

My mother would like to live in the White House if she didn't have to make all the beds.

A loyal citizen,
Paula J.
Age 8
San Francisco

Dear President Reagan:

How old are you?

My mother says you are as old as my grandfather but my grandfather is bald and he can't walk so fast.

Yours truly,
Bobby M.
Age 8
Houston

Dear Pres. Reagan:

Is Mrs. Reagan a good cook?

The First Lady should be the best cook in the U.S.A.

Your friend,
Lois G.
Age 9
Birmingham

Dear President Reagan:

Were you good in spelling in school?

I'm not good in spelling but I would like to be President someday if you don't have to be a good speller.

Yours truly,
Andy H.
Age 8
St. Louis

Dear Mr. President,

I would like to be a Secret Service agent when I grow up.

Right now the only one I protect is my little brother Martin.

A loyal American,
Michael A.
Age 13
Sausalito

Dear Prez,

I like you.

You are a great Prez.

Please send me $10 from the U.S. bank.

Love,
Debbie C.
Age 8
Canton

Dear Pres Reagan,
    I would like to visit Camp David someday.
    I have never been to camp.
    I live in the city.

>   Your friend,
>   *Darlene H.*
>   Age 8
>   Philadelphia

Dear Mr. President,
    I would like to come to the White House and tell you a joke.
    You will like my joke.
    It will make you laugh.

>   Your friend,
>   *Tony W.*
>   Age 9
>   Scranton

P.S. I never made a President laugh before.

Dear Pres Reagan,
    Does the President have a boss?
    Is it God?

>   Love,
>   *Angela R.*
>   Age 8
>   New York

Dear President Reagan:
    I think you should help ex-president Carter.
    Maybe now he could become an actor.

                        Yours truly,
                        Robert H.
                        Age 9
                        Philadelphia

Dear Pres Reagan,

Do you say your prayers every night?
I hope so.

Love,
Mary Ellen G.
Age 10
Dallas

Dear President Reagan,

How old are you?
My mother says you are not supposed to ask
a lady or a President how old they are.

Your friend,
William P.
Age 9
Atlanta

P.S. I am 9.

Dear Mr. President Reagan,

I think you are doing a good job but I don't
know much because I'm just a kid.

Jason K.
Age 10
Providence

Dear President,

I saw Mrs. Reagan on TV.

I liked her dress.

Did you pay for her dress or did you get the money from Fort Knox?

>Your citizen,
>*Valerie M.*
>Age 9
>Stowe

Dear President Ronald Reagan,

Is spanking kids against the law?

Me and my brother would like to know.

>*Alexander and*
>*Michael R.*
>Age 8
>Rochester

Dear President,

We took a poll in our school and you came in second.

>Your friend,
>*Vicky M.*
>Age 9
>Needham

P.S. Robert Redford came in first.

Dear Mr. President,
    How much does a President make?
    I think a President should make a lot of
money even if he gets everything for free.

                          Love,
                          Cara R.
                          Age 10
                          San Francisco

Dear President Ronald Reagan,
    I don't think women should be drafted like
men.
    Women are strong but they don't like blood.

                          A loyal citizen,
                          Debra W.
                          Age 12
                          Houston

Dear Mr. President,
    I think you are very handsome.

                          Love,
                          Mary H.
                          Age 11
                          Bridgton
P.S. Pres Carter was nice looking but you look
better.

104

Dear Pres Reagan:
    I saw a picture of you in a cowboy hat.
    Where will you put your horse when you
live in the White House?

Your citizen,
Jennifer L.
Age 8
Boston

Dear President Reagan,

Will Senator Kennedy ever be President?
Please write and tell me.

Thank you,
Ralph M.
Age 10
Boston

P.S. I won't tell Senator Kennedy.

Dear Pres Reagan,

I'll bet Mrs. Reagan likes the White House a
lot because she doesn't even have to throw out
the garbage.

Eileen J.
Age 10
Greensboro

Dear Mr. President,

I have written you 22 letters.
I can't write any more.
Please answer quick.
I have no more stamps.

Herbert C.
Age 9
Terre Haute

Dear Mr. Pres Reagan,
How come you are so thin?
Are you on a jelly bean diet?

Love,
Julia R.
Age 8
Fort Worth

Dear Mr. President,
I would like to know if Congress is for or against the President.

Love,
Stephanie B.
Age 9
Dayton

Dear President Reagan,
I think you are very brave.
Even when you were shot, you didn't cry.
My sister cries if she gets a splinter in her finger.

Your friend,
Carl J.
Age 10
New Haven

Dear President,
    I would like to fly on Air Force One.
    So far I have only been on a Greyhound bus.

                Love,
                Deena A.
                Age 11
                Cleveland

Dear Mr. President Reagan,
    Is Russia stronger than America?
    Please write if you know the answer.

                Love,
                Rita M.
                Age 9
                Philadelphia

Dear President Ronald Reagan,
    Is it hard to be a President?
    I would like to be sure before I become
President in 2012.

                Your citizen,
                Larry K.
                Age 10
                Peoria

Dear Pres Reagan:

Please write to me and tell me what the Vice President does.

My teacher says not much.

Your friend,
Jerry L.
Age 9
New York

Dear Mr. President,
   Would you rather be Prince than President?
   If you were, Mrs. Reagan could be Princess
Nancy.

                          Your friend,
                          Darlene H.
                          Age 10
                          Miami

Dear President Reagan,
   I like your speeches a lot except the speeches
I don't understand which is most of them.

                          A loyal American,
                          Richard D.
                          Age 9
                          Laguna Beach

Dear Mr. President Reagan,
   Please get rid of the fruit flies in California.

                          Your friend,
                          Mickey H.
                          Age 10
                          Los Angeles

P.S. Maybe you could send them to Alaska where
they will die from the cold.

Dear President Reagan,

Please cut my father's taxes as soon as possible so he can give me a raise in my allowance.

Thank you,
Andy M.
Age 9
Durango

Dear President Ronald Reagan,

We, the students of Grade 6, would like to invite you and Mrs. Reagan to our Halloween party.

The students of
Grade 6
Altoona

P.S. If you can't come, please send the Vice-President or the ex-President Jimmy Carter.

Dear Mr. President,

Do you go to church every Sunday?

I hope you do because the Pres of the United States should be good friends with God.

A loyal American,
Julie K.
Age 10
Akron

Dear Mr. President,
    I hope you will do something to help the poor Americans in the U.S.A. even if you aren't one of them.

                        Thank you,
                        Alexander K.
                        Age 12
                        Detroit

✓ Dear Mr. President Reagan,
    This is letter #5 that I have written to you and so far I still haven't been invited to the White House yet.

                        Love,
                        Leora G.
                        Age 12
                        Reno

Dear Pres Ronald Reagan,
    I would like to keep my money at Fort Knox. I don't think banks are too safe.

                        Yours truly,
                        James K.
                        Age 10
                        Harrisburg

Dear Pres Reagan:
    I heard about you from Walter Cronkite.
                        Your citizen,
                        Allison H.
                        Age 9
                        Nashville

Dear Pres Reagan,

I'm happy you aren't in the hospital anymore.

I prayed for you and so did my father even though he is a Democrat.

> Your citizen,
> *Laurie A.*
> Age 9
> Birmingham

Dear Pres Reagan,

I don't think they should have a draft for the army.

If you want to join the army it should be up to you like when you join the Boy Scouts.

> A citizen,
> *Larry G.*
> Age 10
> Albuquerque

Dear Mr. President,

I baked you a cake.

It is a chocolate cake with ice cream.

I would like to come to the White House and give you the cake soon before the ice cream melts.

> Love,
> *Ellen R.*
> Age 9
> New York

114

Dear President Reagan,

I think Mrs. Reagan looked beautiful at the wedding of Prince Charles.

I'm sorry you didn't have the money to go, too.

> Your citizen,
> *Paula G.*
> Age 11
> Brooklyn

Dear Pres Reagan,

I like you a lot.

I named my cat after you.

> Love,
> *Sara G.*
> Age 8
> Stamford

Dear President Reagan,

Thank you for putting a woman on the Supreme Court.

Maybe someday a woman will be manager of the New York Yankees.

> Sincerely,
> *Mary H.*
> Age 9
> New York

Dear Mr. President,

I am happy you didn't get hurt too much when you were shot.

The Secret Service men are very good.

I wish I could have a Secret Service man at my school.

There is one big kid who always socks me a lot.

Harvey J.
Age 8
Phoenix

Hi Mr. President,

This is Robbie.

I am 8.

I am going to be Pres of the U.S.A.

I'll write you when I'm ready.

Love,
Robbie W.
Age 8
Seattle

Dear Pres Reagan,

I think you are the best President we ever had except for George Washington.

Love,
Susan R.
Age 10
Oakland

P.S. Don't feel bad. Nobody can be better than the father of our country.

116

Dear President Ronald Reagan,

I would like to have my birthday party at the White House.

There will be 15 kids and we won't mess up.

That is why I'm not inviting Freddy.

Your friend,
Renee G.
Age 9
Washington

Dear Pres Reagan,

I think we should have a Be Kind to Animals Week all over the U.S.A.

Nobody does anything for animals and there are more of them than there are of us.

Your citizen,
Ruthellen Y.
Age 9
Richmond

Dear President Ronald Reagan,

Someday your birthday will be a national holiday like Washington, Lincoln and Halloween.

Your friend,
Sharon G.
Age 8
Topeka

Dear Mr. President,

I am glad you cut the budget.
My mother just did the same thing.

Jennifer K.
Age 10
Denver

Dear President,
    I saw a picture of you on a horse.
    Is your horse the first horse of the U.S.A.?

> Love,
> *Wendy M.*
> Age 9
> New York

Dear Mr. President Reagan,
    Thank you very much for helping to end the baseball strike.
    Now could you please help the Chicago White Sox win the pennant?

> Yours truly,
> *Roger W.*
> Age 10
> Chicago

Dear President,
    Is the food at the White House any good?
    The reason I ask is because you look thin and I thought maybe you weren't eating enough.

> Love,
> *Jane R.*
> Age 8
> New Haven

Dear President,

    I like the way you talk.

    For a President you are a good talker.

Your citizen,

Mark H.

Age 9

Sarasota

Dear President Reagan,

    How many rooms are there in the White House?

    I would like to see all the rooms in the White House except the kitchen.

Your friend,

Richard E.

Age 10

Biloxi

Dear Mr. President:

    I read that your favorite food is jelly beans.

    I like jelly beans, too, but my mother won't let me eat them for breakfast.

Nicholas H.

Age 8

Stamford

Dear President Reagan,
  Did you know President Lincoln?
  My best friend Butch said you did.
                    Yours,
                    Davey H.
                    Age 8
                    Albany

Dear Pres Ronald Reagan,
     How are you?
     I am fine.
     What's new with the country?
                         Love,
                         Victoria R.
                         Age 9
                         Hartford

Dear Pres Reagan,
     Do you and Mrs. Reagan sleep in Lincoln's bedroom?
     It must be a very old bed.
                         Love,
                         Judith B.
                         Age 9
                         Reading

Dear Mr. President,
     I'm glad they took good care of you in the hospital.
     My granddad was in the hospital last month and they took good care of him but the bill they gave him almost made him sick all over again.
                         Sincerely,
                         Raphael H.
                         Age 9
                         Boise

Dear President Ronald Reagan,

What does a President do when he isn't President?

Does he do the same things real people do?

Love,
Leslie L.
Age 10
Manhasset

Dear Mr. President,

How many phones do you have in the White House?

We have three phones in our house and my sister uses them all.

Your citizen,
Charles C.
Age 10
Wilmington

Dear Mr. President,

I like your clothes.
You dress very nicely.
Who buys your clothes?
Mrs. Reagan or the F.B.I.?

Love,
Laurie G.
Age 10
Gainesville

Dear President Reagan,
    What is your middle name?
    My teacher said your middle name is Wilson.
    That is a nice middle name.
    I don't even have a middle name.

> *Sherry K.*
> Age 9
> Cleveland

Dear Mr. President,
    My grandmother is in a nursing home.
    She needs help.
    Please help my grandmother.
    Her name is grandmother.

> Love,
> *Betsy H.*
> Age 8
> Wheeling

Dear Mr. Pres Reagan,
    How old do you have to be to be Pres of the U.S.A.?
    I am 10 and I would like to know how long I have to wait.

> *Steve R.*
> Age 10
> Tenafly

124

Dear President,

I heard on TV that your nickname was "Dutch."

I don't have a nickname but my cat does.

Robbie L.
Age 7
Brentwood

Dear Pres Reagan,

I would like to sleep at 1600 Pennsylvania Avenue some night and you can sleep at 420 Main Street some night.

Your friend,
Paul C.
Age 9
Middletown

Dear Pres Reagan,

Me and my best friend, Alex, would like to sing "The Star-Spangled Banner" at the White House.

We know all the verses.

Dennis P.
Age 9
Detroit

Dear Mr. Pres,

I hope you don't build any more nuclear power plants.

They are dangerous.

It is better to go without electric lights than to blow up the world.

Stacey H.
Age 10
Philadelphia

Dear President Reagan,

I think you are a great President if you don't think about it too much.

Your fan,
Leila F.
Age 11
Syracuse

Dear Mr. President,

Please call me on the telephone.

I never had a President call me before.

Your citizen,
Andrew R.
Age 10
Chicago

P.S. You can call me collect.

Dear President Reagan,

You are very lucky to have Mrs. Reagan as First Lady.

She is very smart like Mrs. Johnson and Mrs. Ford and Mrs. Carter.

The First Ladies sometimes are smarter than the Presidents.

Love,
Phyllis K.
Age 9
Baltimore

Dear Mr. President,

    I think one of the reasons you got elected President is because all of the actors voted for you.

Yours truly,
Melissa K.
Age 10
Atlanta

Dear President,

    Someday they will put your picture on a stamp and you will be worth 20 cents.

I like you,
Daphne S.
Age 8
Lake Tahoe

Dear Mr. Reagan,

    I would like to shake your hand.

Jane L.
Age 7
Gary

P.S. If you are too busy I would like to shake the hand of the Vice-President.